Ida Visits 150 YEARS of IDAHO

All aboard to visit Idaho's history!

Written by
Lori Otter and Karen Day
in association with the
IDAHO STATE HISTORICAL SOCIETY
and Illustrated by **Chris Latter**

Ida Jones' Family Tree

Great-Uncle Clarence

Great-Aunt Ida

Great-Uncle Ezra

Great-Uncle Festus

Great-Grandparents

Cousins Rose and Harold

John   **Regina**

Cousin Ralph

Cousin Samuel

Grandparents

Cousin Matilda

Cousin Theodore

Olive   **Jacob**

Cousins Augustus and Flora

Cousin Orwell

Parents

Ann   **Daniel**

Ida Jones

My name is Ida

STATE HORSE
APPALOOSA

STATE FISH
CUTTHROAT TROUT

STATE TREE
WESTERN WHITE PINE

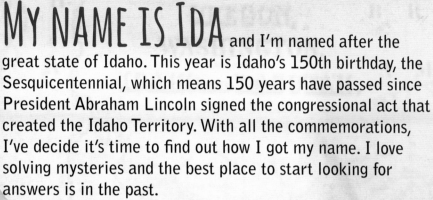

MY NAME IS IDA and I'm named after the great state of Idaho. This year is Idaho's 150th birthday, the Sesquicentennial, which means 150 years have passed since President Abraham Lincoln signed the congressional act that created the Idaho Territory. With all the commemorations, I've decide it's time to find out how I got my name. I love solving mysteries and the best place to start looking for answers is in the past.

I found my first clue in our family album. Everyone has a family history, or ancestry, and every story begins somewhere. Places have a history too and wherever you live becomes part of your story. My family history began back in 1818, but Idaho's story began thousands of years before my family arrived. So that's where this story begins, 10,000 years ago, when mammoths and giant sloths wandered a place that looked very different from the Idaho we know and love today.

STATE FLOWER
SYRINGA

STATE GEM
STAR GARNET

STATE FRUIT
WILD HUCKLEBERRY

STATE MOTTO AND SEAL
"Esto Perpetua"
(Let it be perpetual;
It is forever.)

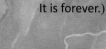

STATE BIRD
MOUNTAIN BLUEBIRD

STATE FOSSIL
HAGERMAN HORSE

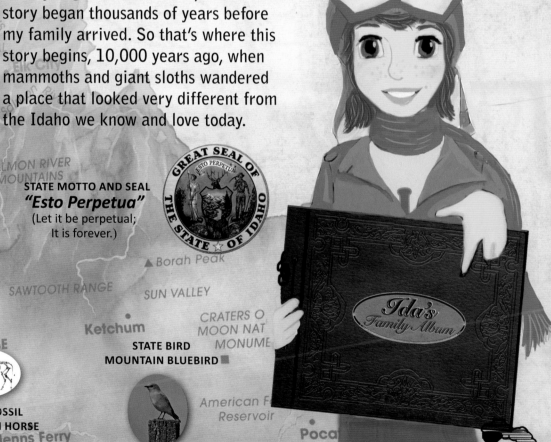

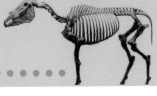

History is like a puzzle; you put it together piece by piece on a solid surface. Think of Idaho's landscape as the place where past events have come together to create this beautiful place and its history. Over millions of years glaciers, volcanoes, earthquakes and floods have shaped this 13th largest state into a land of beautiful extremes. Today, Idaho has 29 mountain ranges, 2,000 lakes and 3,100 miles of river - more than any other state!

Volcanoes created the 400 square miles of blackened, jagged lava fields called Craters of the Moon National Monument near Arco. The last volcano erupted in Idaho 2,000 years ago.

Craters of the Moon

Hagerman Horse

Hagerman Fossil Beds are like Idaho's graveyard, but it's not scary. I saw the skeleton of the Hagerman Horse that lived 3.5 million years ago! By analyzing its bones, scientists know it looked like a zebra with one toe. I even saw bones of a sabertooth cat and giant mastodon! Bring your camera! Thousands of fossil fragments are found every year.

Idaho's 13 national forests, 30 state parks and 12 wilderness areas are home to wolves, bear, fish and one of the nation's largest elk herds in Lolo management zone.

The Salmon River, aka The River of No Return, runs through The Frank Church Wilderness, the largest area of unbroken wilderness in the lower 48 states.

Hells Canyon

Carved by the Snake River, Hells Canyon, formed more than 300 million years ago, is the deepest canyon in North America and serves as the border between Oregon and Idaho.

Shoshone Falls

is often called the Niagara of the West and drops 52 feet farther than Niagara Falls.

One of the most powerful earthquakes in the 20th century made Mt. Borah, 12,662 feet, rise 7 inches on October 28, 1983.

Mt. Borah

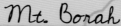

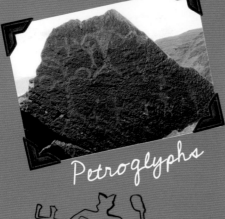

Petroglyphs

Tribes of Idaho

When Christopher Columbus came to North America, he thought he was in India, so he named the Native Americans he met, "Indians."

Archaeologists are scientists who put together pieces of our past. They uncover buried bones, jewelry, weapons, even fragments of preserved food to create a picture of life in earlier times.

These dusty clues confirm Idaho was inhabited 13,000 years ago by the ancestors of the Native American tribes still living in Idaho: Kootenai, Coeur d'Alene, Nez Perce, Shoshone-Bannock and Shoshone-Paiute.

Buhla offers many clues to the story of Idaho's first people.

In 1989, a road crew uncovered ancient human bones near Buhl. Tests proved this woman lived 10,600 years ago, and ate deer, elk and fish. A bone needle and arrowheads were also found. Buhla, as this woman is called, provides many clues to the first people in Idaho.

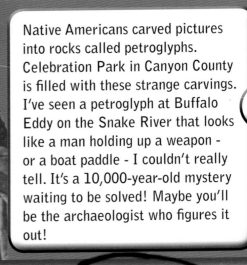

Native Americans carved pictures into rocks called petroglyphs. Celebration Park in Canyon County is filled with these strange carvings. I've seen a petroglyph at Buffalo Eddy on the Snake River that looks like a man holding up a weapon - or a boat paddle - I couldn't really tell. It's a 10,000-year-old mystery waiting to be solved! Maybe you'll be the archaeologist who figures it out!

Native Americans believed the natural world was filled with spirits. They lived in a mystical partnership with their surroundings. Daily life and culture revolved around myths that made animals, plants and the landscape come alive in stories still told today.

Horace P. Axtell

Have you heard the legend of Coyote and Monster? Horace P. Axtell will tell you! GOOGLE this Nez Perce elder and honored storyteller. He won the National Heritage Fellowship in 2008.

The **Nez Perce** called themselves the "Nimiipuu" - or - "the people." Known for their expert horsemanship as hunters and warriors, they were excellent breeders of horses, including the Appaloosa. In 1805, the tribe helped the sick and weary Lewis and Clark expedition recover after an arduous trip over the Bitterroot Mountains.

For centuries, the **Coeur d'Alene** have lived in the Idaho Panhandle. "The Discovered People" as they called themselves, faithfully asked an animal's permission before taking its life on a hunt.

The **Shoshone-Bannock** were once many different tribes with different languages. The northern group was known as the Snake Indians because they carried sticks with snake heads painted on them to scare their enemies. Sacajawea was a Lemhi Shoshone.

The **Shoshone-Paiute** tribes once freely hunted on the land of their forefathers in what is now Idaho, Nevada, and Oregon. Direct descendants of the Northern Paiute today occupy the Duck Valley Indian Reservation of Idaho and Nevada.

The **Kootenai**, or "river people," have never signed a treaty. In 1974, they declared war on the United States - but without guns or violence! Faced with severe economic hardships, the 67 members made this bold move to get international attention to their problems. It worked!

White settlers of Idaho referred to the **Appaloosa** as "a Palouse horse," after the Palouse River, which ran through Nez Perce country. The name gradually evolved into "Appaloosa," Idaho's state horse.

SACAJAWEA

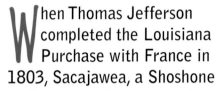

When Thomas Jefferson completed the Louisiana Purchase with France in 1803, Sacajawea, a Shoshone Indian, was a teenage captive of the Hidatsa tribe in North Dakota. A French trapper with a reputation for laziness bought her to be his first wife. Charbonneau was hired by Meriwether Lewis and William Clark to be a guide and interpreter. Sacajawea, a new mother, was allowed to come because she could translate with the Indians and her presence signaled the expedition was peaceful. Women and children never traveled with war parties. Sacajawea is mentioned three dozen times throughout the journals of Lewis and Clark, and each entry describes how this young Indian woman proved more capable and valuable than her husband to the trip's success. Don't forget, Sacajawea was carrying her baby boy on her back every step of the way! At the end of the trip, Charbonneau was paid $500 and Sacajawea earned the respect and appreciation of endless generations of Americans.

At the Sacajawea Center in Salmon, visit Sacajawea's nearby birthplace, see her statue in person, and learn about her place in the history of Idaho and America.

When the expedition reached the Pacific coast, the entire Corps voted where to spend the winter. It was the first time a woman, Sacajawea; and a black slave, York, voted in what would one day become the United States.

LEWIS & CLARK

William Clark

Merewether Lewis

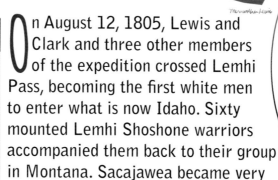

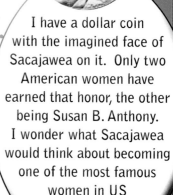

I have a dollar coin with the imagined face of Sacajawea on it. Only two American women have earned that honor, the other being Susan B. Anthony. I wonder what Sacajawea would think about becoming one of the most famous women in US history today?

On August 12, 1805, Lewis and Clark and three other members of the expedition crossed Lemhi Pass, becoming the first white men to enter what is now Idaho. Sixty mounted Lemhi Shoshone warriors accompanied them back to their group in Montana. Sacajawea became very excited, sucking on her fingers, a sign to show these were her people and the chief, Cameahwait, was her brother! A few days later, the entire Corps crossed over Lemhi Pass riding Shoshone ponies gained from Sacajawea's own tribe. The Corps crossed the mighty Bitterroot Mountains at Lolo Pass. The path was steep, the snow deep, and they became so hungry they ate their candles. On September 19, 1805, starving and weak, Clark met the Nez Perce on the Weippe Prairie. About them he wrote, "*These people have shewn much greater acts of hospitality then we have witnessed from any nation or tribe since we have passed the rocky mountains.*" The Nez Perce helped them build dugout canoes to travel on the Clearwater River to the Snake River to the Columbia River and finally, the Pacific Ocean. Historians agree that without the help of both of these Idaho tribes, the Corps of Discovery might never have completed their journey to the Pacific coast.

Lewis took his dog, Seaman, on the expedition. Along the way, the dog was stolen by Indians and Lewis threatened to kill the whole tribe if the dog was not returned. During the two-year expedition, the members ate 263 dogs, but Lewis' Newfoundland was spared.

At the Lewis and Clark Interpretive Center in Lewiston you will see a real tee pee and dugout canoe and relive the explorers' expedition.

Fur Trappers & Explorers

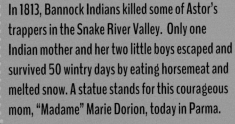

The journey of Lewis and Clark ignited adventurous dreams in many people around the globe. The first to follow those dreams were fur trappers eager to get rich by selling beaver skins called "pelts." David Thompson built the first trading post named Kullyspell House in 1809. John Jacob Astor, a New York City millionaire, hired trappers who came next, gathering furs for Astor to trade with China.

Nathaniel Wyeth arrived after the Astorians and built Fort Hall along the Snake River. He bought furs from mountain men who only left the wilderness to sell pelts and swap stories of escaping from grizzly bears and Indians. The rival Hudson's Bay Company tried to put Wyeth out of business by building Fort Boise and making Idaho a "fur desert."

Summer and winter were a beaver's best friend! In hot weather their pelts were too thin to sell, and in cold weather the ponds were frozen, so mountain men couldn't trap them!

In 1813, Bannock Indians killed some of Astor's trappers in the Snake River Valley. Only one Indian mother and her two little boys escaped and survived 50 wintry days by eating horsemeat and melted snow. A statue stands for this courageous mom, "Madame" Marie Dorion, today in Parma.

First Fort Boise

Fort Hall

Ada and Frank Tingley shown with a five-week catch of coyotes, badgers and bobcats.

During the fur-fashion-craze, 35,000 beaver pelts left Idaho to make top hats and adorn collars. But the beavers were not the only victims. Without the beavers' dams, streams flowed too fast, eroding the land. Trappers traded blankets, guns and trinkets to the Indians for pelts, but they also brought "firewater" and deadly diseases like smallpox. By 1834 the beaver hunt was over, but the search for gold was about to begin.

Why would anyone want a dead beaver sitting on top of their head?

Beaver Hats

Tall, black top hats were the fashion rage in the 1800s. Beaver fur was pressed into a smooth, warm cloth called "felt."

MISSIONARIES

Eliza Spalding

Many churches back East wanted to convert the Indians to Christianity. However, no one asked the Indians if they wanted to become Catholic, Protestant, Methodist or Mormon, which often made missionary work very dangerous. Protestant Henry and Eliza Spalding came first, along with another missionary family, the Whitmans. Working with Nez Perce in Lapwai, the Spaldings built a mission, started a school, brought the first sheep to Idaho, and even planted the first potatoes! In 1837, a daughter, Eliza, was the first white child born in Idaho. Cayuse Indians killed their friends the Whitmans and forced the Spaldings to leave. Today, they're buried near their mission in the Nez Perce National Historic Park near Lewiston.

Cataldo Mission

The oldest building in Idaho.

In 1837, little Eliza was visiting the Whitmans when Cayuse Indians attacked. Many whites were killed and Eliza was kidnapped. The Hudson's Bay Company threatened to stop trade with the Indians unless they freed their hostages. The Whitman massacre ignited a bloody battle between the U.S. military and many tribes, even those tribes that had nothing to do with the massacre.

Next, Father Jean-Pierre De Smet arrived, a Jesuit priest called "The Great Peace Maker" by the Coeur d'Alene. Father Anthony Ravalli followed in 1848 and with the help of Indians, built the Mission of Sacred Heart near the community of Cataldo. The mission still stands today, the oldest building in Idaho. You can see the handprints of the original builders in the adobe walls!

Cousin Matilda was a missionary in Idaho.

THE OREGON TRAIL

Payne's Ferry, near Thousand Springs, an Idaho stop on the Oregon Trail.

Since the journey of Lewis and Clark, people back East had been hearing the land out West was fertile and free. John C. Fremont made a map from Missouri to Oregon that allowed others to follow, but he failed to mention the mosquitoes, dust storms, raging rivers, Indians and accidents that inevitably waited for pioneers along the way. In 1850 alone, 5,000 pioneers died of cholera on the Oregon Trail.

From 1841 - 1866, more than 500,000 made the trek, many were children and most on foot. Catherine Sager was 9 years old when she came through Idaho. A wagon wheel crushed her leg and her mother and father died on the trail, leaving seven brothers and sisters as orphans! They found a home at the Whitman mission until Indians killed the Whitmans and kidnapped her and little Eliza Spalding! When she grew up, Catherine Sager Pringle wrote a book about her difficult journey called, *Across the Plains in 1844*.

Every day was difficult for the westward bound pioneers. This was also true for the Indians who could do little to stop the westward migration across their ancient homelands.

I've seen real wagon ruts of the Oregon Trail at Soda Springs! Imagine walking 400 miles across Idaho on a dirt road in 100 degree heat! The good news was by then your 2,000-mile hike to Oregon was almost over! The bad news was the journey was about to get harder!

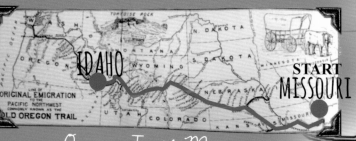

Oregon Trail Map
Between 1841 – 1866, more than 500,000 made the trek.

July 15, 1844

The wagon wheel broke again today. I don't mind stopping - just that it's so hot with no shade trees - just like every day. I fear my ugly freckles will never fade, and my shoes are filled with sand 'cause the soles wore through last month. Father says we must cross the Snake River tomorrow at a place called Three Island Crossing. I'm scared, 'cause I can't swim.

July 16th

Indians! I can see them! They're sittin' on horses on the cliff above the river. There's a boy up there. Wonder what he's thinkin'? Maybe he wants to scalp me - or maybe he just wants to watch me get washed away and drown like poor old Mr. Shaw when his wagon dumped over in the river this morning. Or maybe he just wants to be friends. I wish I could talk to him. No matter what, there's a funeral tomorrow.

July 17th

Happy 11th birthday to me! We made it to Fort Boise! Tonight I had a bowl of molasses pudding, and Old Joe played a lively fiddle 'round the campfire! Only two more weeks of walkin' and we'll be in Oregon!

Regina, 11

Brave Eagle, 11

The sun goes up and down, but the white people do not stop their long walk. Their wagons follow the path of long scars the others left behind. There are many young ones, like the girl I see today. I think she is wearing a war bonnet.

Her animals are big as elk and devour the earth. There is no more sweet grass for our horses, and our fathers ride for seven moons to find the buffalo. This is my 11th summer and I will ride with the warriors on the buffalo hunt. Father says the buffalo may now be eight moons away I do not understand the white language so I cannot ask her why she is here or where the wagons are going. I can only hope they do not stay. This is the birthplace of my many grandfathers. We cannot leave their spirits behind. Many warriors say the whites will go back where they came from if we fight. I do not know what a new moon will bring – except more wagons. Soon I will do a vision quest. Perhaps the wolf, the bobcat and fox can tell me how to bring back the sweet grass and buffalo.

STRIKE IT RICH

The Nez Perce spoke of finding stars in rocks that gleamed like eyes of the Great Spirit. In 1860, Elias Pierce set off with a few prospectors and the daughter of a Nez Perce chief as a guide to determine if these legends of gold were true. The problem was that the U.S. government had granted the land around the Clearwater River to the Nez Perce in the Treaty of 1855. Whites were not welcome. When 3 cents worth of gold washed into one of the prospector's pans, it was the beginning of Idaho's Gold Rush. Within a year, approximately 7,000 men had moved into the new town of Pierce.

Idaho Prospectors
Thousands of miners poured west into Nez Perce territory beginning in 1860.

Prospectors kept pouring into Nez Perce territory and new strikes happened throughout. Thousands found nothing but dirt while many discovered nuggets worth $100! Towns sprang up and disappeared as prospectors followed the newest shout of "Gold!" For a few months, Florence was the richest town in the United States, but now it's only home to ghosts. Lewiston, named for Meriwether Lewis, boomed with steamboat traffic, gambling parlors, THE GOLDEN AGE newspaper and celebrities like Wyatt Earp. Even with its fancy French restaurant and brand new school, the rough-and-tumble town saw few women and children.

A father teaches his young son about gold mining.

Ida's instructions on HOW TO STRIKE IT RICH!

$$$$$

1. Dip your gold pan into a shallow part of a stream and scoop up gravel.
2. Swirl the pan around and around, washing the gravel with water, careful not to spill everything.
3. Gold is heavier than dirt so it will settle at the bottom of the pan.
4. Go directly to a candy store to spend your $$!

WESTWARD IDAHO

Florence was the richest town in the United States, but now it's only home to ghosts.

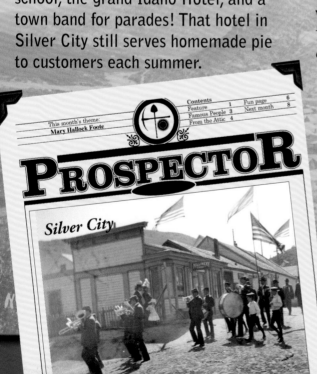

Lewiston boomed with steamboat traffic.

Great-Uncle Ezra's Ghost

Miners moved on to Boise Basin and Yankee Fork. By 1864, Idaho City had produced more gold than the town of Florence. Opera singers and the town band frequented its concert hall, but the audience was mostly male since the census counted only 450 women and 250 children among 7,000 men! Silver City welcomed families and bragged a two-story school, the grand Idaho Hotel, and a town band for parades! That hotel in Silver City still serves homemade pie to customers each summer.

Idaho City produced more gold than Florence and hosted opera singers in the concert hall.

In 3 years, Idaho had produced more than 30 million dollars in gold and silver, but it was still lacking two important things: law and order.

Prospectors called gold dust "flour gold" because it was soft as flour - or - "Oro Fino" in Spanish. The gold is gone but the town of Orofino remains!

This month's theme:
Mary Hallock Foote

Contents			
Feature	1	Fun page	6
Famous People	3	Next month	8
From the Attic	4		

PROSPECTOR

Silver City

WANTED
Diamond Field Jack

820

DEAD OR ALIVE

Diamondfield Jack bragged he got paid $150 a month by cattlemen to shoot sheepherders. Suspected of killing two, he was sentenced to hang. While waiting execution, two other men confessed and Jack was granted a reprieve the day before he was scheduled to swing by his neck!

OUTLAWS

In 1896, Butch Cassidy rode in Montpelier, Idaho, robbed the bank without firing a single shot. The Sundance Kid was not along for the ride, but he and Butch eventually rode into Hollywood history.

...was a common command in early mining camps. In rugged places without laws and sheriffs to enforce them, guns made the final decision in everything from card games to mining claims. Shady characters pedaled fake gold dust. Miners with real gold might never make it to the assay office to cash in their riches. Robbers sometimes hit stagecoaches more than once in a day. Outraged citizens banded together to chase down these criminal elements by ending violence with violence. William J. McConnell and the Payette Vigilantes led the way to successfully establishing law and order. From 1863 to 1896 eleven men were tried in their court and hanged. McConnell went on to become a U.S. Senator in 1890 and Idaho's third elected Governor in 1893.

FUN FACT: Congress was in the middle of the Civil War when it created the Idaho Territory in 1863 and forgot to immediately transfer rule of U.S. law. In 1866, the Idaho Supreme Court ruled that a man convicted of a crime while there was no law did not commit that crime because there was no law against what he did. All felons convicted during the first year of Idaho Territory's existence (March 3, 1863 – March 4, 1864) were freed.

IDAHO SCENIC BYWAY MARKER 27.5: Chinese Hanging Tree Chinese immigrants were 80% of the population in Pierce until 1870. People were worried the Chinese were taking over Idaho. This site marks a trail used by an angry band of vigilantes who accused five Chinese men of murdering merchant, D.W. Fraser. There was no trial.

It's a tough job, but somebody's got to do it!

ON THE PATH TO WAR

The trespassing of thousands of gold miners on Nez Perce lands enraged and saddened the Indians. To make matters worse, in 1863 the U.S. government decided to reduce the size of the tribe's reservation lands and ordered the tribe to a small reservation around Lapwai. Many Nez Perce leaders were disgusted by white men's lies and refused to sign what they call the "Steal Treaty." This led to the Nez Perce War of 1877.

On a cold, January morning in 1863, U.S. soldiers attacked and killed hundreds of Shoshone women, children and warriors in one of the worst massacres of Native Americans in U.S. history. A monument stands today as a reminder of the Bear River Massacre.

All over the West, Native Americans were struggling to survive. Sacred lands were buried under boomtowns. Diseases killed the old and young, erasing the tribes' past and future. Horses, pigs, cattle and sheep were devouring camas bulbs and chokecherry that Indians used for food and medicines. Beaver, antelope, elk and buffalo had disappeared. To avoid starvation, many tribes were reduced to begging food from settlers. Whites made treaties then broke them. Angry warriors took scalps and revenge in the Whitman massacre and the Nez Perce, Snake, Sheepeater and Bannock wars. However, by 1880, all tribes in Idaho had been forced onto reservations.

President Lincoln strictly forbade, "cruelty ... and the infliction of suffering upon the American Indians ..." but, he was embroiled in the Civil War and thousands of miles away from western battlefields like Bear River.

Chief Joseph

At White Bird, 70 Nez Perce won a battle against a larger foray of 120 U.S. soldiers. Chief Joseph tried to escape by walking 1,600 miles to Canada with his tribe. He was stopped 30 miles from the border. Freezing and hungry Chief Joseph showed his great strength as a leader and surrendered with his famous speech. "My heart is sick and sad. From where the sun now stands, I will fight no more forever."

MARCH 4, 1863

Junior

PROSPECTOR

IDAHO BECOMES A TERRITORY

Hello Idaho! Goodbye Washington Territory! Crowds roared in Lewiston when they heard the 37th U.S. Congress had officially approved the existence of the Idaho Territory on March 4, 1863. President Abraham Lincoln signed the legislative act that same day. The President appointed William H. Wallace our first Governor. Governor Wallace is presently traveling from Washington, DC, to Lewiston, our new capital city. He will arrive in three or four months after a coast to coast journey by steamer via 30 overland miles of the Panama Isthmus.

William H. Wallace
Lincoln's nickname for Governor Wallace was "Old Idaho."

1863

1853

The State of Idaho went through many changes to become the shape and size it is today. The area began as part of the Oregon Territory until Oregon became a state and then, it merged into the Washington Territory. Ten years later, Idaho Territory boasted a land mass bigger than Texas and included parts of current-day Wyoming, Montana and Yellowstone Park!

(Great-Aunt) Ida Jones, Reporter

Idaho's map did not morph into its modern shape until England finally relinquished its holdings in 1868. Imagine, the Queen of England once ruled part of the Gem State! She must have been looking for more "crown jewels."

ABE IN IDAHO?

Could the Governor of the Idaho Territory have saved President Lincoln's life on April 14, 1865? No one will ever know since Wallace declined the President's invitation to the Ford Theatre that fateful evening.

March 4, 2013 Idaho celebrated the SESQUICENTENNIAL (150th Anniversary!) of Lincoln signing the Territorial Act.

The 16th President never had the chance to visit the great territory he helped create in 1863, but his legacy lives on in Idaho, a state that would not exist without his dedication.

President Lincoln was sleepless from stresses of the Civil War on the night he created the Idaho Territory. Hundreds of thousands of Americans, Union and Confederate soldiers alike, were dying in the battle to end slavery. Lincoln needed money to win and end the war, and Idaho was filled with gold and silver. Plus, the President wanted to ensure slavery would never exist out West. He lobbied Congress until they approved his proposal after midnight on the final day of the session. Lincoln stayed awake to sign the handwritten document at 4 o'clock in the morning, March 4, 1863. Twenty-seven years later, President Benjamin Harrison signed another congressional act making Idaho the 43rd state.

See Abe's real signature at the Lincoln Legacy Exhibit at the Idaho State Archives!

The oldest Lincoln statue west of the Mississippi stands in front of the Boise Capitol.

Abraham Lincoln

BOISE : A NEW CAPITAL

Second Fort Boise

Five months after Lincoln created the Idaho Territory, the U.S. Army built Fort Boise at the intersection of the Oregon Trail and roads to thriving mining camps like Silver City and Idaho City. The Commander and eight homesteaders then drew up a ten-block city plan on the north side of the river. In 1864, the gold rush population had shifted to southern Idaho, so Boise was named the new capital.

The residents of Lewiston were angry and armed men locked the State Seal and records in jail until federal troops were sent in to bring the papers to Boise. The second governor, Caleb Lyon, snuck out of Lewiston in the middle of the night in a row boat! The State Seal arrived in Boise the same day Lincoln was assassinated.

By 1868, Boise's dirt streets were lined with 1,658 citizens and 400 structures, half of them residential. The new capital quickly rivaled Idaho City as a center of agriculture, business, learning and culture.

Boise's dirt streets were lined with 1,658 citizens and 400 structures.

Idaho's first capitol in Lewiston.

IN 1863, 725 people lived in Boise and Lewiston had a population of 7000. By 1864, the gold rush town of Idaho City had almost 7,000 people and Lewiston's population was estimated to have declined by half. Gold or the lack of it was the determining factor in the development of early cities.

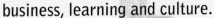

22

Boise has always been the most geographically isolated capital city in the United States. The end of the gold rush limited growth until 1890, when Idaho became a state. A canal irrigation project resumed that year, creating jobs and an agricultural boom. The desert that had been snubbed by hundreds of thousands of Oregon Trail pioneers suddenly became a promise land. In six months, the population doubled to 4,000 and never stopped growing. Today, the City of Trees is home to over 200,000 people. Idaho remains primarily an agricultural state, but ranching, transportation, education and technology provide a vibrant economy for more than 1.6 million people.

Today's Boise is home to more than 200,000 people.

A French guide of early explorer, U.S. Army Captain Bonneville, named the city after crossing hundreds of miles of desert and coming upon the deep green Boise River valley. "Les Bois! Les Bois!" he exclaimed, "The trees, the trees!"

You can still travel on the Oregon Trail in Boise. All you have to do is drive down historic Harrison Boulevard.

The search for riches in Idaho attracted many immigrants to Idaho. Boise became a home to differing cultures, religions and ethnicities, including Chinese, Mexican, African American, Basque and more. These varying traditions created a rich and sustaining cultural diversity in Idaho then and now.

"Ni Hao" — "Hello" From The Chinese

The 1870 census in Idaho listed 4,269 Chinese men (one-third of the total population) and most were named "Ah" -- Ah Saw, Ah Wait, etc., etc. Whites did not speak Chinese and assumed they all had the same first name. This was one of many cultural misunderstandings that created challenges for the Chinese in Idaho. "Ah Saw" means, "This one is Saw."

They'd heard America was "a mountain of gold." Very poor, most signed lifetime contracts of servitude for passage to the California gold rush and beyond. In almost every Idaho town, they worked long hours, cooking, washing laundry, carrying water and building railroads to send a few dollars to their families back in China. Life was difficult for the Chinese in Idaho and often, white settlers and miners made it more so. In some areas, white miners could work claims for free, while Chinese had to pay $6 a month! Soon, they were prohibited by law from owning claims at all!

Polly Bemis

Polly Bemis was only 53 inches tall, but she was tough as any mountain man. In China, her poor family sold her into slavery and she was sent to San Francisco in a cage. She was sold again for $2,500, and finally befriended by Charlie Bemis in Warren, Idaho. They wed and lived on a remote homestead on the Salmon River. She died in 1933 and the Polly Bemis House became a historical museum. A book and movie called *A Thousand Pieces of Gold* made her famous.

Despite hardships, they kept their customs alive, living together in Chinatowns and celebrating traditions like the Chinese New Year with parades that continue today. Looking back, it's clear the Chinese helped build Idaho and their contributions deserve the respect they worked so hard to earn long ago.

I visited the Polly Bemis House when my family rafted the Middle Fork of the Salmon River! You can see where she nursed a cougar back to health!

HOLA! IDAHO

Jesus Urquides

Hardworking Mule Team

As cattle ranching expanded into the Treasure Valley, so did the number of Vaqueros, or Mexican cowboys. The 1870 census included 60 Mexican-born individuals and most of them, whether a vaquero, mule packer or businessman, knew Jesus Urquides.

Hard-to-reach mining camps depended on mule teams to bring supplies. It was dangerous work, guiding strings of mules over rocky shale mountain passes packed with everything from pianos to food, but Jesus Urquides was the best and his mules the quickest. One of his mules became famous for carrying 600 pounds of steel cable! He came to Boise in 1863, transporting goods to Silver City, Atlanta and Challis. In 1879, he built the Spanish Village at 115 Main Street in Boise to house his workers. Idaho life agreed with Urquides, who was still lean and packing at 93 years old! He died at the age of 95 and is buried, along with many of Boise's first residents in Pioneer Cemetery on Warm Springs Avenue.

Manuel Fontez

discovered galena, the most important lead ore mineral, near Clayton. Fontez Creek still carries Manuel's name.

"¡Buenos dias amigos!" I'm learning to speak Spanish at the Hispanic Cultural Center of Idaho, in Nampa!

THEN CAME YORK

Africans were brought to America as slaves. Before the Civil War, only free black or escaped slaves came west unless brought by their owners. William Clark's servant, York, was the first to enter Idaho with their expedition in 1805. He was a source of fascination for the Indians who sometimes tried to rub the black off his skin.

James Beckwourth

James Beckwourth, a freed slave, arrived in Idaho in 1824. A mountain man, he wrote a book about his adventures trapping, surviving capture by the Crow Indians, and marrying the daughter of a chief. Beckwourth Pass in California, which he discovered during the Gold Rush, is named for him.

In the 1880s the railroad in southern Idaho hired many African Americans. During this migration, prejudice by whites prohibited them from buying property or sending their children to public schools. Yet many African Americans prevailed and stayed in Idaho. By 1900, 940 African Americans had settled here.

"Aunt Viney" Moulton, a freed slave who crossed the plains barefoot in 1867, became the first black to be a member of the Boise Presbyterian Church.

Tracy Thompson

One-third of western cowboys in the 1800s were African American. Tracy Thompson became a famous champion rodeo rider. His grandson was elected the first black mayor of Pocatello.

Today in Boise, Idaho's Black History Museum preserves and educates about African American heritage and culture in Idaho and celebrates notables like jazz musician, Gene Harris.

The Great Pyrenees dog is named after the mountains where the Basque race originated. Large and loyal, they were bred for hundreds of years as guard dogs for sheep. The Basques brought them to Idaho and you can still see them herding flocks today.

JAIALDI!

The Basques are one of the oldest living ethnic groups from Europe, but they've never had a country of their own. Therefore, they became seafarers and settled on many continents - including North America. No matter where they went, including Idaho in the 1880s, the Basques kept their culture strong.

When people think of Basques in Idaho, they think of sheepherding. But they first came as miners and saw a great opportunity as sheep ranching expanded across the territory. They mastered the outdoor lifestyle and quickly began inviting family members to come from Spain to join them. Presently, Idaho has one of the biggest Basque populations in the U.S., and they maintain and celebrate their culture and heritage with international festivals like JAIALDI in Boise every five years.

I saw the Basque folk dancers perform at the San Inazio Festival! They can kick to the sky in Boise!

The oldest surviving brick building in Boise is THE CYRUS JACOBS - UBERUAGA BOARDING HOUSE. It boasted the city's first indoor bathtub and served as the wedding site of Idaho's famous Senator William Borah. See this building and many historic Basque families' names chiseled on the sidewalks of Grove St.!

HOMESTEADING IDAHO

Everyone worked on the homestead. Chores were done before children were allowed to play. Dolls were made of corn husks and sticks were used for sword fighting.

CORN HUSK DOLL

Many historians say the West was settled by "The Homestead Act" of 1862. President Lincoln pledged 160 free acres to anyone who could make the land produce in five years. This sounded easy enough to the hundreds of thousands of people who migrated west on his promise. They soon discovered that "proving up" the arid soil of southern Idaho was as difficult as farming dry cement. The northern land of the Palouse didn't need irrigation, so it was more productive. However, the Idaho Territory was still dealing with Indians, outlaws and harsh winters. Even the poorest families from foreign countries now had the chance to own their own home, raise livestock and vegetables, hunt and fish and chop wood to stay warm -- but "easy" it was not. By 1881, irrigation and railroads began building a better future for Idaho.

My Cousin Augustus and his wife Flora were homesteaders. They lived in a one-room house with their six children and without glass windows, electricity or running water—even in the winter! Can you imagine living your whole life without TV and video games?

Cousin Augustus and wife Flora at their farm.

READING, WRITING AND DIRT FLOORS...

Today in Idaho there are still 10 "one-teacher" schools. In 1880, there were not many more than that. In pioneer days, the floor was dirt and the teacher might be younger than the oldest pupil and taught all the grades together. Books and paper were expensive, so everyone did their work on a tiny blackboard called a slate. Some children had to walk hours to school and mostly in the winter, since spring, summer and fall were the busy times for planting and harvesting on the farm.

The Morrill Land Grant College Act of 1862 gave Idaho 90,000 acres of federal land to create a university. Moscow won the bid to host the University of Idaho. The honor helped ease northern citizens' anger over the capital being moved to Boise.

I went to Outpost Days in Murphy and sat inside the old one-room school. My iPad didn't get reception, so we watched a horned toad race instead of reading!

Remember the Spaldings who founded the Lapwai mission? Mrs. Spalding started the first school in Idaho in 1834.

There were 1,239 white children in Idaho in 1865 and only 427 of them were attending school. By 1889, almost 12,500 children were in Idaho schools!

In 2014, the one-room school in Tendoy will celebrate its 100th birthday!

Cousin Flora taught her own six children and five more in this one-room schoolhouse.

Keep Them Dogies Rollin'!

Gold miners needed food, and many settlers decided to make a living by ranching. They mostly raised cattle and sold the meat and hides, but chickens, pigs and sheep were also tasty and dairy cows provided milk and cream. From then until now, agriculture became big business in Idaho.

Cattlemen and sheepherders competed for rangeland to feed their stock. Wars over grazing rights were fought with guns and lawyers. Cattlemen were angry that sheep ate the grass to stubs and polluted watering holes. But the cost of raising sheep was less and selling their meat and wool was very profitable. Some cattlemen hired men like Diamondfield Jack to shoot sheep and their herders. More than 50 people and 53,000 sheep died in this conflict, but the invention of barbed wire in 1870 was the beginning of the end of the wide open range. Today, both cattle and sheep ranching offer a prosperous way of life for many Idaho families.

How can you tell one steer from another? Cowboys burn marks, called "brands" into their hides. I don't have any cattle, but I do have my own Ida Jones brand! I use it to roast marshmallows.

● Every October, thousands of sheep parade down the main street in Ketchum. The Trailing of the Sheep is one of the oldest traditions in the Wood River Valley, with plenty of mutton stew, Basque music and national sheepdog trials.

● Idaho's fast-growing population demanded more beef. Giant herds of cattle came in "drives" from as far away as Texas. Somebody had to keep the steers, "dogies" moving. That's where the cowboys came in!

BUCKAROOS

"Welcome To Our West"

Governor C. L. "Butch" Otter
in the 2012 Caldwell Night Rodeo!

Spanish cowboys, called vaqueros, started cattle herding on horseback in Mexico, Texas and California long before Idaho even saw a steer in the 1860s. Today, lassos and chaps are thought of as rodeo accessories, but these began as a cowboy's tools on the long cattle drives that brought ranching to Idaho. Movies show cowboys singing around the campfire, but the job was very difficult. Imagine sitting in a saddle ten hours a day, every day, in every kind of weather. Indians, stampedes and rustlers posed constant dangers. And nobody won a trophy for staying on a bucking horse! You rode it ... or you walked!

Jackson Sundown,

a Nez Perce Indian, was born the year Idaho became a territory. A legendary cowboy, he was 53 years old when he won the World Title in the Saddle Bronc Championship in 1916.

Bonnie McCarroll

is Idaho's most famous cowgirl. Born in 1897 near Boise, she won the Cowgirl World Championship before being fatally injured in 1929. The Pendleton Round-Up dangerously required women's stirrups tied together for bronc riding. Bonnie's boot got caught and the horse rolled. In 2006, Bonnie was inducted into the National Cowgirl Hall of Fame.

"... We cowgirls that like the game well enough to play it should play it just like the cowboys do. Why, I'd feel insulted ... if I was told to tie my stirrups down!"
Bonnie McCarroll

In 1912, my cousin Orwell rode in the first rodeo in Idaho in Grangeville. Broncs still buck in the Border Days rodeo every July.

Cousin Orwell was an old cowhand

THE DESERT BLOOMS

I n northern Idaho, naturally-rich soil made wheat grow thick and tall. Towns like Moscow prospered in the Palouse area. In southern Idaho's desert, where less than 10 inches of moisture fell, homesteaders had to do "dry farming." Some near the Snake River dug ditches that carried water to the fields, called irrigation, but that water couldn't reach thousands of acres. The Carey Act of 1894 gave Western states a million federal acres to sell at about $25 an acre to cover the cost of developing irrigation projects. Within two years, the Snake River Plain turned green with plants for the first time since the Hagerman Horse wandered it, 65 million years ago. Irrigation sent Idaho on its way to becoming an agricultural giant.

Cousin Rose and husband Harold

Picking Fruit

Arrowrock Reservoir

Arrowrock Dam was the highest in the world when it was completed in 1915.

Apple and cherry orchards became productive businesses. Sugar beets and barley did well too. And of course, potatoes flourished all over southern Idaho.

Viticulture is the raising of grapes to make wine. More than 50 wineries are making southern Idaho the new "wine country" of America.

Idaho organic farming is growing and produces over $30,000,000 a year in Idaho.

The top four agricultural exports of Idaho can be found in your kitchen right now: dairy, beef, potatoes and wheat.

Idaho and potatoes go back much further than J.R. Simplot and McDonald's Golden Arches. Remember Reverend Spalding at Lapwai Mission in 1836? He was the first to grow potatoes in Idaho. Next, Mormon pioneers discovered the warm days and cool nights produced more potatoes than they could eat and began selling to California. Idaho spud-lovers should next thank Luther Burbank, the scientist who in 1872 cross-bred the Russet Burbank, the potato that loves Idaho!

In 1917, Joe Marshall was the first to create Idaho "spud fever." He took his giant potatoes to a Chicago restaurant chain and by 1937, Mr. Marshall was as successful as his delicious spuds and helped create the Idaho Potato Commission. In the 1950s, J.R. Simplot built his spud empire by patenting methods to dehydrate potatoes and flash-freeze French fries. He sold these tasty inventions to the U.S. Army and McDonald's, making him the oldest billionaire in America when he died in 2008 at age 99.

The Potato Market

Today, every Idahoan would need to eat 63 potatoes a day to eat all the potatoes grown here each year! That's a whole lot of French fries!

She'll be Coming 'Round the Mountain

The Transcontinental Railroad took six years to connect Sacramento to Omaha, Nebraska. In 1874, train tracks were laid from Utah into the first town in Idaho - Franklin and beyond. Towns throughout the Snake River Valley like Montpelier, Pocatello and Caldwell grew in size and comforts from the arrival of the Oregon Short Line and Union Pacific.

Northern Pacific

By 1882, the Northern Pacific was steaming across northern Idaho to and from Spokane. Rathdrum, Sandpoint, Lewiston and Moscow all grew from the supplies and people being transported. Trains also carried miners headed for Wallace and Kellogg and the great lead silver mining strikes of 1884. With rail connections, Idaho entered national markets with ore, grain and timber. Then, in 1889, several predecessor railroads merged to form the Great Northern that stretched from Minneapolis across Idaho to Seattle. Covered wagons still rolled across the plains for two more decades, but trains forever changed Idaho's wild frontier.

Northern Pacific

Many historic railways eventually became part of the BNSF (Burlington Northern Santa Fe). Today, BNSF freight trains speed across northern Idaho daily, hauling everything from A to Z — including autos to apples to live elephants from Barnum & Bailey's Circus! Amtrak passengers glide across BNSF tracks with a beautiful view of Lake Coeur d'Alene. In Hauser, 200 Idahoans conduct the business of ensuring all these trains run safely and on time. The environment benefits too. Each BNSF freight train takes 500 trucks and their emissions off the highways.

REMEMBER THE RULES OF THE RAILS!

Cousin Ralph, conductor

AND OPERATION LIFESAVER REMIND YOU . . .

1 The only safe place to cross is at a designated public crossing with a crossbuck, flashing red lights or a gate. If you cross at any other place, you are trespassing and can be ticketed or fined. Cross tracks ONLY at designated pedestrian or roadway crossings.

2 Railroad tracks, trestles, yards and equipment are private property and trespassers are subject to arrest and fine. If you are in a rail yard uninvited by a railroad official you are trespassing and subject to criminal prosecution; you could be injured or killed in a busy rail yard.

3 It can take a mile or more to stop a train, so a locomotive engineer who suddenly sees someone on the tracks will likely be unable to stop in time. Railroad property is private property. For your safety, it is illegal to be there unless you are at a designated public crossing.

4 Trains overhang the tracks by at least three feet in both directions; loose straps hanging from rail cars may extend even further. If you are in the right-of-way next to the tracks, you can be hit by the train.

5 Do not cross the tracks immediately after a train passes. A second train might be blocked by the first. Trains can come from either direction. Wait until you can see clearly around the first train in both directions.

6 Flashing red lights indicate a train is approaching from either direction. You can be fined for failure to obey these signals. Never walk around or behind lowered gates at a crossing, and DO NOT cross the tracks until the lights have stopped flashing and it's safe to do so.

7 Do not hunt, fish or bungee jump from railroad trestles. There is only enough clearance on the tracks for a train to pass.

Trestles are not meant to be sidewalks or pedestrian bridges! Never walk, run, cycle or operate all-terrain vehicles (ATVs) on railroad tracks, right-of-ways or through tunnels.

8 Do not attempt to hop aboard railroad equipment at any time. A slip of the foot can cost you a limb or your life. If you see a train coming STEP BACK and WAIT!

9 Be aware trains do not follow set schedules. Any Time is Train Time!

10 CROSSING TRACKS ON A BICYCLE REQUIRES CAUTION AND EXTRA ATTENTION! Narrow wheels can get caught between the rails. If possible, walk - don't ride - across. Always cross at a 90-degree angle. And remember, rails are slippery when wet!

BNSF Railway is an active participant in Operation LifeSaver, a national organization dedicated to increasing rail-safety awareness and reducing train/vehicle and pedestrian collisions.

Know your SIGNS and SIGNALS! You wouldn't play in the water if there were sharks around, so don't play on or around tracks! Anytime is train time!

35

TIMBER!

Idaho Lumberjacks

Mines needed sturdy beams so tunnels would not cave in. Towns needed lumber for homes, schools and sidewalks. Railroads needed ties to keep expanding. For a time, the growing demand for lumber seemed as endless as Idaho's white pine forests.

In the early 1900s, Frederick Weyerhäeuser sent men from the Great Lakes to scout Idaho's forests. These lumberjacks lived in remote camps. Their muscles powered saws that cut down "King" trees 425 feet tall and six feet across. Logs were floated downriver to barges or sawed into smooth boards and hauled by trains. The work was dangerous and paid $3.40 a day with $1.20 taken for camp costs. Families arrived. Towns like McCall, Sandpoint, St. Maries and Coeur d'Alene prospered. The biggest white pine sawmill in the world was built in Potlatch in 1906.

I plant a baby tree (seedling) each April on Arbor Day. Did you know one tree produces 260 pounds of oxygen a year?

The timber industry helped northern Idaho's economy flourish, but at a high cost. Clear-cutting stripped thousands of acres of trees and caused land erosion. Wildlife, fish and rivers suffered. People realized the forests needed to be preserved and kept healthy. Today, Idaho's forests are carefully harvested and replanted for the future.

James Stevens, born in Weiser, wrote the tall tales of lumberjack Paul Bunyan and Babe, the Blue Ox.

FIREFIGHTING

In the summer of 1910, the Idaho Panhandle caught fire. Three million acres burned in two days! Ed Pulaski was a firefighter who saved the lives of his crew by forcing them, with a revolver, to stay in a mine shaft while the forest burned around them. He is famous for inventing the firefighting tool that works like an ax and a hoe. "The Pulaski" is still used by firefighters!

WAGON WHEELS TO WINGS!

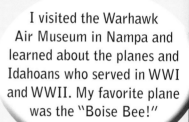

21·032
IDAHO POTATOES - 1928

Picture these devices in your mind — a covered wagon, stagecoach, steamboat, train, cable car, bicycle, car and an airplane. People have always wanted to move faster, safer and more comfortably, so modes of travel evolved quickly in 200 years. But all of this forward movement in history, called progress, also required roads, canals, docks, tracks and runways that needed wood, metal and lumber. Transportation also requires energy from muscles, wind, water, steam or an engine and people to design, build and manage it. Looking at the old Oregon Trail ruts next to Interstate 84 today, it's easy to see the important role transportation plays in Idaho's past, present and future.

It is said that Idaho got its name from a steamboat.

The state of Idaho issued its first plates in 1913, with the price determined by the value of the vehicle. There were only 2,083 plates issued that year.

I visited the Warhawk Air Museum in Nampa and learned about the planes and Idahoans who served in WWI and WWII. My favorite plane was the "Boise Bee!"

FOR "UR" INFORMATION

Pacific Express telegraph office, Lewiston

Texting on a cellphone, it's hard to believe that when your grandmother was a child all communication required person-to-person delivery – even if the information was written! But it's even harder to believe the first cellphone was invented by Michael Faraday in 1843!

Benjamin Franklin, first postmaster, 1775

After pioneers settled out west, most never traveled more than 50 miles from their home. Mail service was the only way to communicate. Ben Franklin was the first postmaster in 1775 and by 1828, there were 7,800 U.S. post offices. Before the completion of the Transcontinental Railroad, however, letters took two to three months to arrive in Idaho from back east! No wonder Indians relied on smoke signals!

In 1862, Idaho's first electric light was switched on at the Philadelphia Smelter near Ketchum.

In 1955, Arco became the "First City in the World to be lit by atomic power." The electricity was generated by nuclear energy.

Idaho's first phone service started in Hailey in 1883. Switchboard operators used to plug in wires to connect calls and many people talked on the same "party line!"

See Spot Run

In 1919, Philo Farnsworth was 13 years old. He was plowing straight lines on his family's Idaho farm and got the idea of breaking down images into parallel lines of light and transmitting them as electrons to a screen. Eleven years later, he invented the television!

The 43rd State

George L. Shoup

Twenty-seven years after President Lincoln signed the Idaho Territorial Act, President Benjamin Harrison signed papers creating the State of Idaho. Everywhere in Idaho, bands played, fireworks lit up the sky, and parades and crowds filled the streets as a 43rd star was added to every flag in America. George L. Shoup from Salmon was elected the first Governor and became Idaho's first U.S. Senator just 2 months later.

Statehood brought a new set of challenges. Northern residents had wanted to be part of Washington Territory and often disagreed with elected officials from southern Idaho. Then, in 1892, the Coeur d'Alene mine war turned bloody. Miners wanted safety and better pay so they organized a strike and stopped working until conditions were improved. Owners hired other people to work, so angry miners dynamited the Frisco Mill. Troops arrived to prevent more violence. Governor Frank Steunenberg was murdered, and the alleged conspirators were tried in Idaho's Trial of the Century.

Emma Edwards

Emma Edwards was only 18 when she became the first and only woman to create a state seal. Idaho's motto is Esto Perpetua, Latin for "It is perpetual."

In 1890, only men voted to elect Governor Shoup, but Idaho was the 4th state to give women the right to vote in 1896 -- 24 years before the 19th Amendment was passed! Suffrage Movement leaders like Susan B. Anthony and Abigail Scott Duniway worked hard to earn all women the right to vote!

William Borah

William Borah became internationally famous prosecuting the leaders of the Western Federation of Mines in the Governor's murder. Known as "the Lion of Idaho," he later served as a U.S. Senator and ran for President in 1936. Mount Borah is named after him.

A Cultural Snapshot

Mary Hallock Foote drew scenes of pioneer life in Idaho.

The word culture means the language, religion, art, music and traditions of a particular group of people. For example, the Nez Perce culture is as different from the Coeur d'Alene Indians as American culture is from the Chinese. Idaho's culture is made up of Hispanic, Native American, Chinese, African American, Basque, Euro-American cultures and more—which makes us a diverse and colorful community!

Idaho has inspired many great writers.

Ernest Hemingway
FOR WHOM THE BELL TOLLS

Edgar Rice Burroughs
TARZAN

Vardis Fisher
MOUNTAIN MAN

Silver City had the first theater in Idaho.

Payette-born Harmon Killebrew was inducted into the Baseball Hall of Fame. Kirsten Armstrong won two Olympic gold medals in cycling in 2008 and 2012.

Nell Shipman was a silent filmmaker. She lived at Priest Lake with a zoo of wild animals that starred in movies like, "A Bear, A Boy and A Dog."

Great-Uncle Clarence acted at Silver City's theater.

Gutzon Borglum, an Idaho sculptor, spent 14 years chiseling the faces of four presidents into Mount Rushmore!

Boise's Symphony Orchestra can trace its roots to the Boise City Orchestra of 1885.

SURVIVAL VS. FUN

Lewis and Clark would be amazed if they saw Idaho today. Almost every outdoor activity necessary for their survival now offers opportunities for outstanding outdoor recreation opportunities.

Fishing was a main food source for many Native American tribes and settlers. Trout, steelhead and Chinook salmon still provide food and fishing fun for all ages.

The Corps of Discovery walked, boated and rode horses 1,800 miles to the Pacific. Every summer, thousands hit the trails for exercise and fresh air in Idaho's wilderness areas and parks.

Snowshoes and skis would have aided the Corps' snowy mountain crossings. Imagine what they would think riding a chair lift to the top of Baldy Mountain in Sun Valley!

I went white water rafting on the River of No Return and had a great time! Too bad Lewis and Clark couldn't come along!

Hunting was once essential to survival and now, it's a skillful and regulated hobby that helps manage animal populations.

TODAY'S HUNTER in Idaho

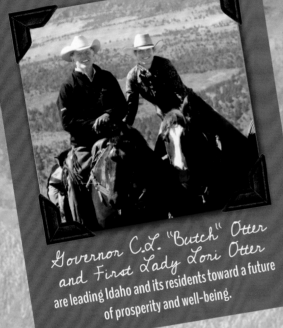

Governor C.L. "Butch" Otter and First Lady Lori Otter are leading Idaho and its residents toward a future of prosperity and well-being.

I daho has it all: breathtaking scenery, abundant wildlife, plentiful water and natural resources, four fabulous seasons, endless opportunities for outdoor recreation, dynamic cities, enterprising rural communities, excellent schools, diverse ethnicities with vibrant cultures, outstanding elected leadership and a prosperous business economy. Much has changed in the 150 years since Abraham Lincoln put his name on the Idaho Territory Act in 1863, but the most important fact about Idaho remains the same; there's no better place to call home!

- Micron, Hewlett Packard and Idaho National Laboratory create cutting-edge technology and employ thousands of Idahoans.

- Preserving the state's sterling environment is a top priority for Idaho's citizens and leaders.

- Southern Idaho offers perfect testing ground for large-scale alternative energy sources like wind farms.

- Idaho's rugged beauty and recreational activities attract 20 million tourists annually.

Looking back at the last 150 years of Idaho, it's clear to me why my family chose the Gem State. We Idahoans have a proud past and a promising future. I'm IDA and I'm lucky to be named after the great state of Idaho!

Ida's Family Album

Dear Ida and Children of Idaho,

   Can you believe it? The Idaho Territory is 150 years old! Happy Birthday to us! That sure seems ancient, but really, Idaho, which began as the Idaho Territory in 1863, is pretty young compared to other states! Some states have trees older than our Gem State. Still, Idaho has come a long way in a short time! From Lewis and Clark to iPads and iPods, the world and Idaho are in a new place and moving forward every day.

   It is fun to reflect back on all the opportunities and things that we have today that our ancestors didn't have. For example, imagine life without your family car! I don't know about you, but I have a lot of respect for the Idahoans who contributed all their talents, time and treasure to make this great state what it is. Looking around at all the advantages our forefathers helped create, I have to ask myself: What are we going to do to make Idaho a better place for future generations?

   The word citizenship means it's our responsibility to use our talents to help others. We all have special gifts and blessings that we can contribute to our Idaho and our world. One way to discover how others have used their talents is to look back at your family history and your state's history. Ida has learned that her family included a reporter, a mountain man, farmers, and a pilot! I hope you take the time to look at your history and learn how your family helped shape your life today with their yesterdays. Most of all, I'm hoping you'll discover how you can make a difference in your lifetime. Perhaps someday, you'll be the next governor…maybe even the first girl governor of our great state! And this year, you can be a good citizen by finding a way to join in the celebrations of Idaho's 150th birthday.

   The Governor and I look forward to reading about all your adventures and contributions to our state now and in the future … and I BET we won't have to wait 150 years for you to make Idaho and the world an even a better place to live! Just remember our state motto, "Esto Perpetua," which means, "It is forever!" The Governor and I hope Idaho will be with you forever, and she will always call you home to her wherever life may take you.

Warm regards,

Lori J. Otter
First Lady of Idaho

1. From 1863 to 1890, the Idaho Territory had 16 governors, four who never set foot in Idaho.

2. Our "Gem State" produces 72 types of precious and semiprecious stones.

3. One of the largest diamonds ever found in the U.S., nearly 20 carats, was discovered near McCall.

4. The prototype of the first nuclear submarine, Nautilus, was built and tested in the desert near Arco.

5. In 1926, the world's first alpine skiing chairlift, located in Sun Valley, cost 25 cents per ride.

6. Astronauts used Craters of the Moon National Monument as a training ground for moon walks.

7. The serpent-like Bear Lake Monster, witnessed by several different people, was first sighted around 1868 and measured 90 feet in length. Some people still refuse to night fish there.

8. The revolutionary Scott Ski Pole was invented by Ketchum's Edward Scott.

9. The most recent, largest and deepest volcanic rift in the U.S. is located in south central Idaho.

10. Silverwood, the Pacific Northwest's largest theme park, is located in Athol.

11. The longest single-state gondola in the world is located in Kellogg.

12. Lava Hot Springs was a sacred gathering place for the Shoshone-Bannock Indians.

13. The Snake River is said to be named after the Snake Indians.

14. President Jefferson actually sent Lewis and Clark to look for waterway to the Pacific called the NORTHWEST PASSAGE. None existed.

15. William Clark adopted and schooled both of Sacajawea's children after her death.

16. Larry Echo Hawk, Idaho's first Native American Attorney General, was appointed by President Obama to serve as the leader of the U.S. Bureau of Indian Affairs.

17. One sockeye salmon returned to Redfish in 2001. A total of 648 sockeye returned in 2010.

18. Beaver tails are very good eating.

19. The Malad River got its name from Donald Mackenzie after his exploration party got sick eating beavers that were digesting poisonous roots along that river.

20. There are four Indian Reservations in Idaho - the Coeur d'Alene, Lapwai, Fort Hall and Duck Valley, plus the Kootenai Territory.

21. The first Jewish synagogue built in Boise stood on the corner of State St. and 11th for 100 years. In 2001, it was moved to the Morris Hill Cemetery and is still regularly used for worship.

22. A Jefferson Peace medal was discovered in 1899 near the Potlatch River. One of the coins given by Lewis and Clark to the Nez Perce, it was returned to the tribe in 1968.

23. "Queen of Diamonds," Kitty C. Wilkins, was a legendary beauty who became rich and famous as the boss of the Diamond Ranch with 5,000 horses and 40 men.

24. In 1862, Captain John Mullan built the first civilian-engineered road in the Pacific Northwest. Much of Interstate 90 follows his trail above Lake Coeur d'Alene.

25. Legend says the Bunker Hill Mine in Kellogg was discovered by a mule named Old Bill!

26. The Owyhee Mountains are named for Hawaiian men that got lost with Mackenzie's exploration in 1818.

27. Idaho is said to be named after the steamboat IDAHO that ran on the Columbia River in 1860, not the sternwheeler IDAHO that paddled on Lake Coeur d'Alene in 1903.

28. Boise's first airport was built in 1926 with a gravel runway where BSU is located..

29. Electric trolleys ran on the streets of Boise from 1891 -1928.

30. Ben Halliday established the first stagecoach line in Idaho in 1864 that eventually became part of Wells Fargo Stageline.

31. Family is so important to the Nez Perce that they have 180 different words for relatives.

32. Idaho's first public school opened in Florence with six students.

33. The O'Farrell cabin, the first in Boise, still stands on Fort Street.

34. After the Civil War ended many Confederate democrats didn't like Lincoln and moved west. They were called "copperheads" in Idaho.

35. Chief Joseph's name translates to "Thunder Rolling Down the Mountain."

36. Trappers hid pelts underground until they could pack them out of the wilderness. These furry buried treasures were called "caches." That's how Cache Valley got its name!

37. Walt Disney's wife Lillian was born in Spalding and grew up on the Nez Perce Indian Reservation in Lapwai. Lillian is credited with having named her husband's most famous character, Mickey Mouse, in 1928.

38. Idaho was the first state in the U.S. to elect a Jewish governor, Moses Alexander, in 1914.

39. Arco was the first city to be lit by Atomic Energy, in July 1955.

40. The Hagerman Valley produces nearly 85% of all commercial trout sold in the U.S.

41. Lincoln's bodyguard, Ward Hill Lamon, ran unsuccessfully to become the governor of Idaho.

42. News traveled slowly in 1863. The tri-weekly Statesman did not report Lincoln's death until April 27th, 13 days after the assassination.

43. During the Great Depression, a group of artists called the "Hobohemians," formed the Boise Art Association, now the Boise Art Museum.

44. You can see four states from Heaven's Gate Lookout located at the Seven Devils' Peaks mountain range.

45. Idaho Territory's public school system was established in 1864.

46. The town of Rigby is referred to as the birthplace of television.

47. Bad cooks in Idaho logging camps were called "gut robbers."

48. In 1972, Idaho became the first state in the U.S. to ratify the Equal Rights Amendment!

49. The tallest single-structure sand dune in North America stands 470 feet high and is located at Bruneau Dunes State Park.

50. It is against the law to give an Idahoan a box of candy which weighs more than fifty pounds.

WORD SEARCH IDAHO HISTORY

Find these 20 words. Put them in the correct spaces of the timeline below and discover Idaho's historical timeline from prehistoric times to today.

APPALOOSA
BEAVER
BOISE
CATALDO
CHINESE
CIVIL
FRANKLIN
GOLD
LEWISTON
LINCOLN

MULE
OREGON
OTTER
PETROGLYPHS
POTATO
RAILROAD
SALMON
SHOSHONE
SPALDING
STATE

```
E W O F N J E K S L X A N S U
T V X B N S P P E Q S B L H I
A P R Z E O P W V O T L O P D
T F B N T A I A O H M Q C Y S
S Y I A C S V L L P Q F N L O
W H T X T D A E O D D R I G R
C O M O X P F P R T I A L O E
O C N O P S H O S H O N E R G
W D D A O R L I A R F K G T O
S A L M O N L I V I C L A E N
E E B A R O P C E M G I J P G
F V X E T G O L D S U N A Z K
Y X T R W A I R U M I L W G R
C T N B G S C X N E E O E Z C
O D G Z L K Y Q P T V R B W J
```

4,500 BC Indians made rock carvings called _____ .

1800 AD Sacajawea was a _____ Indian.

1805   Lewis and Clark traveled the River of No Return, aka _____ .

1805   The _____ was bred by the Nez Perce and is Idaho's state horse.

1832   Mountain men trapped _____ .

1839   The first white settler of Idaho was _____ .

1842   The _____Mission is the oldest building in Idaho.

1845   Covered wagons traveled the _____ Trail.

1860   The first white settlement in Idaho was _____ .

1860   You need a_____pan to find it!

1863   President _____created the Idaho Territory.

1863   America was fighting the_____ War .

1863   Idaho Territory's first capital city was _____ .

1864   The capital city was moved to _____ .

1869   The Transcontinental _____ ___ __crossed America.

1872   Polly Bemis was a famous _____pioneer in Idaho.

1884   Noah Kellogg's _____found silver at Bunker Hill.

1890   Idaho becomes the 43rd _____.

1917   The _____becomes Idaho's famous vegetable .

2013   The _____is a water animal and Idaho's Governor.

46

Idaho State Song
Verses by Albert J.Tompkins
Chorus by McKinley Helm
Music by Sallie Hume-Douglas
Arranged by Craig Chernos

Here We Have Idaho

Lyrics

You've heard of the wonders our land does possess,
Its beautiful valleys and hills.
The majestic forests where nature abounds,
We love every nook and rill

Chorus:

And here we have Idaho,
Winning her way to fame.
Silver and gold in the sunlight blaze,
And romance lies in her name.
Singing, we're singing of you,
Ah, proudly too. All our lives thru,
We'll go singing, singing of you,
Singing of Idaho.

There's truly one state in this great land of ours,
Where ideals can be realized.
The pioneers made it so for you and me,
A legacy we'll always prize.

Chorus:

And here we have Idaho,
Winning her way to fame.
Silver and gold in the sunlight blaze,
And romance lies in her name.
Singing, we're singing of you,
Ah, proudly too. All our lives thru,
We'll go singing, singing of you,
Singing of Idaho.

You can listen to
this music online at
http://gov.idaho.gov/about/song.html

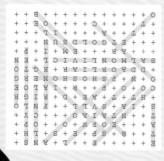

Word Search Solution

47

Special Thanks to:

The Idaho Community Foundation, Idaho State Historical Society, Foundation for Idaho History, Governor C.L. "Butch" Otter, Senator Jim Risch and Office, Idaho State Commerce and Tourism Department.

Idaho State Historical Society (ISHS) Image Credits

Inside front cover (background image, Silver City picnic, 60-139.17); **4.** *Craters of the Moon #66-13.6;* **6.** *Petroglyphs; Coeur d'Alene Tribe #76-2.52G;* **7.** *(Left to Right) Shoshoni children dancing #78-2.66; Nez Perce woman with children #63-221.125a; Nez Perce man on horse with teepee #663;* **10.** *Fort Hall, #1254d ; Fort Hall, #189B3;* **11.** *Trapping Ada and Frank Tingley #83-75;* **12.** *Eliza Spaulding #77-2.22;* **13.** *Payne's Ferry #885;* **16.** *Caswell brothers, miners #73-57.18; Boy gold panning #77-105.2;* **17.** *Steamboat "Idaho" #78-208.160; Idaho City 1874 #78-129.25D; Silver City parade 1898 #60-139.6; (Background image: Silver City #878);* **18.** *Diamondfield Jack #77-2.33;* **19.** *Chief Joseph #691;* **20.** *William Wallace #1331; Maps of Idaho Territory 1860, 1863, 1867;* **21.** *Abraham Lincoln #477c;* **22.** *(Military) Fort Boise Image #75-68-1; Territorial Capitol Lewiston #2710; Boise Main St. 1866 #73;* **24.** *Low Family, Idaho City #75-189.3; Polly Bemis #62-44.1; Chinese New Year Parade #79-148.2;* **25.**

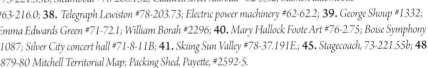

Apple Packing Shed, near Payette, 1907

Urquides pack train #247q; **26.** *Elvina Moulton #78-48.1; James Beckwourth #76-2.86; Tracy Thompson #80-83.2;* **27.** *Oinkara Basque dancers #64-114.5 and #64-114.11;* **28.** *Homesteads #70-71.28 and #78-164.56; Potatoes photog. by Bisbee #73-221.1662;* **29.** *Midway School #79-38.7; Lost River School #61-118.3;* **30.** *(Background image: Cowboys Snake River #1133);* **31.** *Jackson Sundown, Indian rodeo;* **32.** *Payette Fruit Orchard #74-75.12; (Background image: Harvesting #78-37-156);* **33.** *Idaho Falls "Spud Alley" #64-109.2;* **34.** *Winter train #65-128.39a;* **36.** *Lumbering #73-79.4;* **37.** *Stagecoach photog. By Bisbee #73-221.55B; Steamboat #78-208.152; Caldwell street railroad #62-53.2; Salmon automobile #63-216.0;* **38.** *Telegraph Lewiston #78-203.73; Electric power machinery #62-62.2;* **39.** *George Shoup #1332; Emma Edwards Green #71-72.1; William Borah #2296;* **40.** *Mary Hallock Foote Art #76-2.75; Boise Symphony #1087; Silver City concert hall #71-8-11B;* **41.** *Skiing Sun Valley #78-37.191E.;* **45.** *Stagecoach, 73-221.55b;* **48.** *1879-80 Mitchell Territorial Map; Packing Shed, Payette, #2592-S.*

1879-80 Mitchell Territorial Map of Idaho

Additional non-ISHS Image Credits

1. *(Background image, train, BNSF Railway);* **3.** *State horse, flower, etc., State of Idaho;* **4.** *Hagerman Horse, National Park Service;* **5.** *Elk, Idaho Tourism, #4354; Hells Canyon, Idaho Tourism, #2206; Shoshone Falls, Idaho Tourism, #5418; Mt Borah, Idaho Tourism, #3938;* **8.** *Sacajawea Center in Salmon, Idaho Tourism, #4057;* **11.** *Beaver Hats, Jefferson National Expansions, nps.gov;* **12.** *Cataldo Mission, Idaho Tourism, #6263;* **18.** *Butch Cassidy, Creative Commons, Wikipedia;* **19.** *Bear River Massacre photo, Idaho Department of Transportation;* **21.** *Boise Capitol building, State of Idaho; Lincoln statue, unknown;* **23.** *Boise Skyline, Idaho Tourism, Peg Owen;* **25.** *Jesus Urquides, University of Idaho #3-0746a;* **30.** *Sheep, from collection of Carol MacGregor, PhD – Photographed by Laura MacGregor Bettis;* **31.** *Gov. C.L. "Butch" Otter at Caldwell Rodeo; Bonnie McCarroll, unknown;* **32.** *Arrowrock Reservoir, Idaho Tourism;* **33.** *Truck with potato, Idaho Potato Commission;* **34.** *Northern Pacific Train, BNSF; Modern train, BNSF;* **37.** *License plate, Idaho Department of Transportation;* **38.** *Benjamin Franklin, National Portrait Gallery, public domain;* **40.** *Mount Rushmore, Wikipedia, Creative Commons;* **42.** *Wind farms, Idaho Tourism; Rafting, Idaho Tourism; Gov. C.L. "Butch" Otter and First Lady Lori Otter, State of Idaho;* **43.** *Letter, Lori Otter, State of Idaho;* **44.** *Gondola, Idaho Tourism;* **48.** *Jack Tendoy, Library of Congress.*

Published by I-Zing Books. Boise, Idaho. Printed in China.

Jack Tendoy, Library of Congress